W9-CNH-836

DISCARD

And God Bless Me

DISCARD

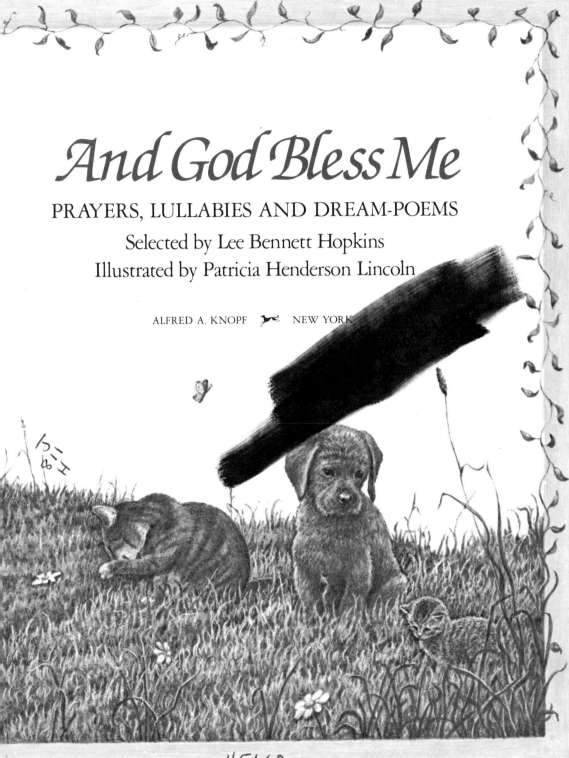

And God Bless Me

PRAYERS, LULLABIES AND DREAM-POEMS

Selected by Lee Bennett Hopkins

Illustrated by Patricia Henderson Lincoln

ALFRED A. KNOPF NEW YORK

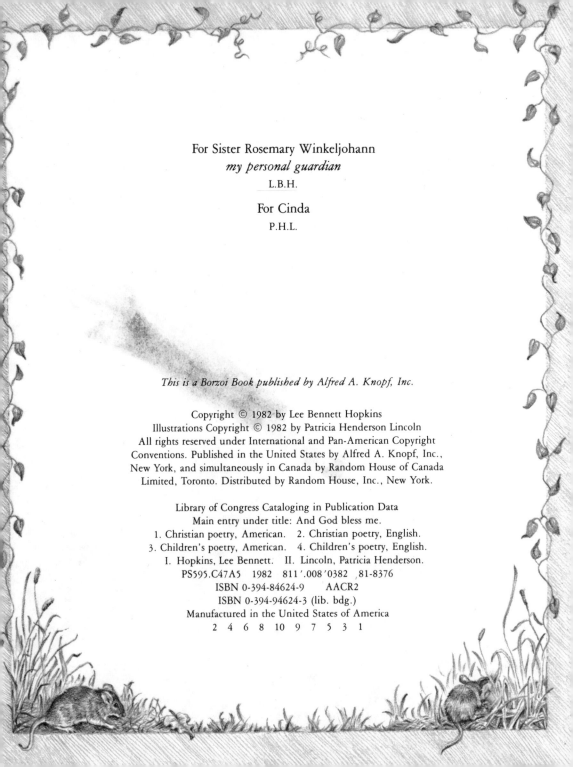

For Sister Rosemary Winkeljohann
my personal guardian
L.B.H.

For Cinda
P.H.L.

This is a Borzoi Book published by Alfred A. Knopf, Inc.

Copyright © 1982 by Lee Bennett Hopkins
Illustrations Copyright © 1982 by Patricia Henderson Lincoln
All rights reserved under International and Pan-American Copyright
Conventions. Published in the United States by Alfred A. Knopf, Inc.,
New York, and simultaneously in Canada by Random House of Canada
Limited, Toronto. Distributed by Random House, Inc., New York.

Library of Congress Cataloging in Publication Data
Main entry under title: And God bless me.
1. Christian poetry, American.   2. Christian poetry, English.
3. Children's poetry, American.   4. Children's poetry, English.
I. Hopkins, Lee Bennett.   II. Lincoln, Patricia Henderson.
PS595.C47A5   1982   811′.008′0382 ,81-8376
ISBN 0-394-84624-9   AACR2
ISBN 0-394-94624-3 (lib. bdg.)
Manufactured in the United States of America
2   4   6   8   10   9   7   5   3   1

Acknowledgments

Every effort has been made to trace the ownership of all copyrighted material and to secure the necessary permissions to reprint these selections. In the event of any question arising as to the use of any material, the editor and the publisher, while expressing regret for any inadvertent error, will be happy to make the necessary correction in future printings.

Grateful acknowledgment is made to the following for permission to reprint the copyrighted material:

Thomas Y. Crowell, Publishers, for "Good Night" from *In One Door and Out the Other* by Aileen Fisher. Copyright © 1969 by Aileen Fisher. By permission of Thomas Y. Crowell, Publishers.

Curtis Brown, Ltd. for "Nighttime" by Lee Bennett Hopkins. Copyright © 1977 by Lee Bennett Hopkins.

Barbara M. Hales for "Gentle Prayer." Used by permission of the author who controls all rights.

Harcourt Brace Jovanovich, Inc. for "Names" by Carl Sandburg. Copyright © 1953 by Carl Sandburg. Reprinted from his volume *The Sandburg Treasury: Prose and Poetry for Young People* by permission of Harcourt Brace Jovanovich, Inc.

Harper & Row, Publishers, Inc. for "Moon/Have you met my mother? . . ." from *Near the Window Tree: Poems and Notes* by Karla Kuskin. Copyright © 1975 by Karla Kuskin. By permission of Harper & Row, Publishers, Inc.

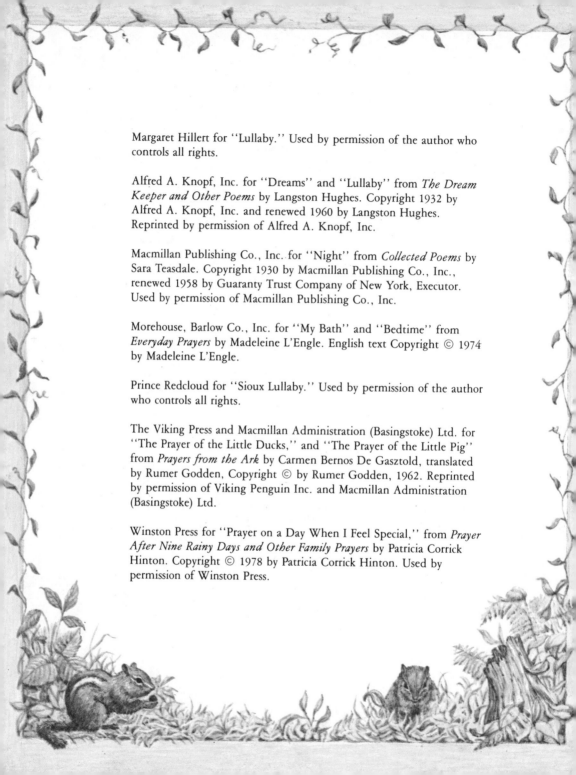

Margaret Hillert for "Lullaby." Used by permission of the author who controls all rights.

Alfred A. Knopf, Inc. for "Dreams" and "Lullaby" from *The Dream Keeper and Other Poems* by Langston Hughes. Copyright 1932 by Alfred A. Knopf, Inc. and renewed 1960 by Langston Hughes. Reprinted by permission of Alfred A. Knopf, Inc.

Macmillan Publishing Co., Inc. for "Night" from *Collected Poems* by Sara Teasdale. Copyright 1930 by Macmillan Publishing Co., Inc., renewed 1958 by Guaranty Trust Company of New York, Executor. Used by permission of Macmillan Publishing Co., Inc.

Morehouse, Barlow Co., Inc. for "My Bath" and "Bedtime" from *Everyday Prayers* by Madeleine L'Engle. English text Copyright © 1974 by Madeleine L'Engle.

Prince Redcloud for "Sioux Lullaby." Used by permission of the author who controls all rights.

The Viking Press and Macmillan Administration (Basingstoke) Ltd. for "The Prayer of the Little Ducks," and "The Prayer of the Little Pig" from *Prayers from the Ark* by Carmen Bernos De Gasztold, translated by Rumer Godden, Copyright © by Rumer Godden, 1962. Reprinted by permission of Viking Penguin Inc. and Macmillan Administration (Basingstoke) Ltd.

Winston Press for "Prayer on a Day When I Feel Special," from *Prayer After Nine Rainy Days and Other Family Prayers* by Patricia Corrick Hinton. Copyright © 1978 by Patricia Corrick Hinton. Used by permission of Winston Press.

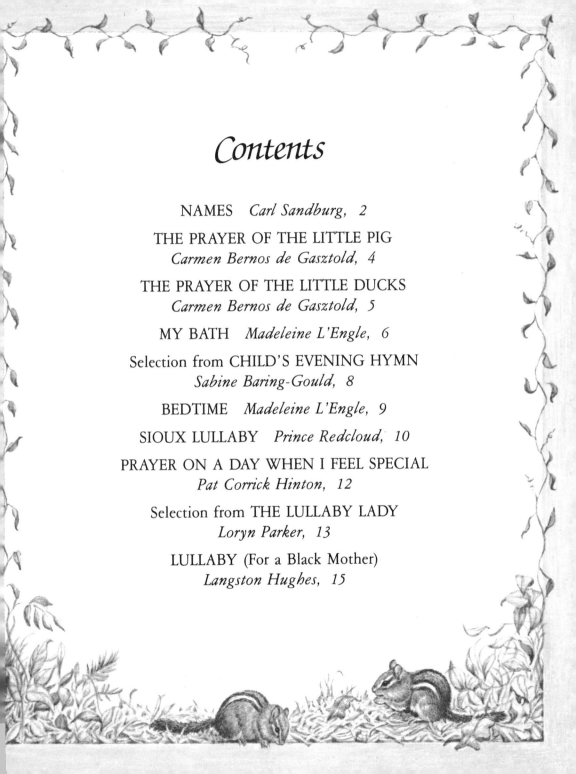

Contents

NAMES   *Carl Sandburg, 2*

THE PRAYER OF THE LITTLE PIG
Carmen Bernos de Gasztold, 4

THE PRAYER OF THE LITTLE DUCKS
Carmen Bernos de Gasztold, 5

MY BATH   *Madeleine L'Engle, 6*

Selection from CHILD'S EVENING HYMN
Sabine Baring-Gould, 8

BEDTIME   *Madeleine L'Engle, 9*

SIOUX LULLABY   *Prince Redcloud, 10*

PRAYER ON A DAY WHEN I FEEL SPECIAL
Pat Corrick Hinton, 12

Selection from THE LULLABY LADY
Loryn Parker, 13

LULLABY (For a Black Mother)
Langston Hughes, 15

MOON *Anonymous, 16*

Selection from NEAR THE WINDOW TREE
Karla Kuskin, 16

LULLABY *Margaret Hillert, 17*

GENTLE PRAYER *Barbara M. Hales, 19*

DREAMS *Langston Hughes, 20*

NIGHTTIME *Lee Bennett Hopkins, 21*

NIGHT *Sara Teasdale, 22*

GOOD NIGHT *Aileen Fisher, 23*

And God Bless Me

There is only one horse on the earth
and his name is All Horses.
There is only one bird in the air
and his name is All Wings.
There is only one fish in the sea
and his name is All Fins.
There is only one man in the world
and his name is All Men.
There is only one woman in the world
and her name is All Women.
There is only one child in the world
and the child's name is All Children.
    There is only one Maker in the world
    and His children cover the earth
    and they are named All God's Children.

NAMES, *Carl Sandburg*

*L*ord,
their politeness makes me laugh!
Yes, I grunt!
Grunt and snuffle!
I grunt because I grunt
and snuffle
because I cannot do anything else!
All the same, I am not going to thank them
for fattening me up to make bacon.
Why did You make me so tender?
What a fate!
Lord,
teach me how to say

Amen

THE PRAYER OF THE LITTLE PIG
Carmen Bernos de Gasztold

4

*D*ear God,
give us a flood of water.
Let it rain tomorrow and always.
Give us plenty of little slugs
and other luscious things to eat.
Protect all folk who quack
and everyone who knows how to swim.

Amen

THE PRAYER OF THE LITTLE DUCKS
Carmen Bernos de Gasztold

5

My bath is the ocean
and I am a continent
with hills and valleys
and earthquakes and storms.
I put the two mountain peaks of my knees
under water and bring them up again.

Our earth was like that—
great churnings and splashings,
and continents appearing and disappearing.

Only you, O God, know about it all,
and understand, and take care
of all your creation.

MY BATH, *Madeleine L'Engle*

*D*ay is over,
    Night draws high,
Shadows of the evening
    Steal across the sky.

Darkness gathers,
    Stars begin to peep;
Birds and beasts and flowers
    Soon will be asleep.

from CHILD'S EVENING HYMN
Sabine Baring-Gould

*G*ood night.

Good night daylight
and playing trains;
good night books,
and bread and butter,
and games of make believe,
and brothers and sisters
and father and mother.

Good night, God.
Take care of us while we sleep,
and you have a good night, too.
Amen.

BEDTIME
Madeleine L'Engle

*S*leep, *mi su-la*,

little brother,

sleep,
sleep,
sleep.

Dream dreams, *mi su-la*,

little brother—

strong dreams,
brave dreams,
dreams so deep—

as you sleep, *mi su-la*,

little brother,

sleep,
sleep,
sleep.

SIOUX LULLABY, *Prince Redcloud*

*F*ather,
thank you
for letting me
be me.

You made me special.

No one else
is just like me.

No one ever will be
just like me.

I'm going to give you
a special gift today.

It's me.
Amen.

PRAYER ON A DAY
WHEN I FEEL SPECIAL
Pat Corrick Hinton

12

*H*ave you heard of the Lullaby Lady,
Who lives on a cloud, snowy white;
Where she sits making songs for the children,
By the rays of the moon, all the night?

from THE LULLABY LADY
Loryn Parker

My little dark baby,
My little earth-thing,
My little love-one,
What shall I sing
For your lullaby?

Stars,
Stars,
A necklace of stars
Winding the night.

My little black baby,
My dark body's baby,
What shall I sing
For your lullaby?

Moon,
Moon,
Great diamond moon,
Kissing the night.

Oh, little dark baby,
Night black baby,

Stars, stars,
Moon,
Night stars,
Moon,

For your sleep-song lullaby!

LULLABY (For a Black Mother)
Langston Hughes

I see the moon,
And the moon sees me;
God bless the moon,
And God bless me.

MOON
Anonymous

*M*oon
Have you met my mother?
Asleep in a chair there
Falling down hair.

Moon in the sky
Moon in the water
Have you met one another?
Moon face to moon face
Deep in that dark place
Suddenly bright.

Moon
Have you met my friend the night?

from NEAR THE WINDOW TREE
Karla Kuskin

Near and far, near and far,
Over the hill there hangs a star.
Over the star is a slice of moon,
And a cloud will cover them very soon.
Far and near, far and near,
My teddy and I are dreaming here
And over us both my mother is bending,
Crooning a tune without any ending,
Near and far, near and far,
Over the hill there hangs a star.

LULLABY
Margaret Hillert

17

A gentle prayer is what I'll say
To close this peaceful, gentle day.

With gratitude that I have heard
The pre-dawn chirpings of a bird.

With thankfulness that I have seen
The many hues of summer-green.

With a singing heart that I could feel
The soft warm grasses when I kneel.

With love for those who give me care
I softly close my gentle prayer.

GENTLE PRAYER, *Barbara M. Hales*

*H*old fast to dreams
For if dreams die
Life is a broken-winged bird
That cannot fly.

Hold fast to dreams
For when dreams go
Life is a barren field
Frozen with snow.

DREAMS
Langston Hughes

*H*ow do dreams know
      just when to creep

Into my head
      when I fall off to sleep?

NIGHTTIME
Lee Bennett Hopkins

21

*S*tars over snow,
    And in the west a planet
Swinging below a star—
    Look for a lovely thing and
        you will find it,
It is not far—
    It never will be far.

NIGHT
Sara Teasdale

This day's done.
Tomorrow's another.

Good night, Daddy.
Good night, Mother.

Good night, kitten,
book, and brother . . .

In one dream
and out the other.

GOOD NIGHT
Aileen Fisher

LEE BENNETT HOPKINS
is the editor of several highly-acclaimed poetry
anthologies including *Elves, Fairies, & Gnomes* and
Go to Bed!, as well as two novels for young people,
Mama and *Wonder Wheels,* all published by Knopf.
He holds advanced degrees from Kean College of
New Jersey, Hunter College, and the Bank Street
College of Education. A member of the Board of
Directors for The National Council of Teachers of
English, he chaired the 1978 Poetry Award
Committee.

Mr. Hopkins lives in Scarborough, New York.

PATRICIA HENDERSON LINCOLN
grew up in Plainfield, New Jersey, and attended Mary
Washington College in Fredericksburg, Virginia. Her
illustrations have appeared in *Yankee Magazine* and
Reader's Digest. This is her first illustrated children's
book.

Ms. Lincoln lives in Longmeadow, Massachusetts.

PUBLIC LIBRARY MEM. (POUND RIDGE)

3 1026 10 15247 9

DISCARD